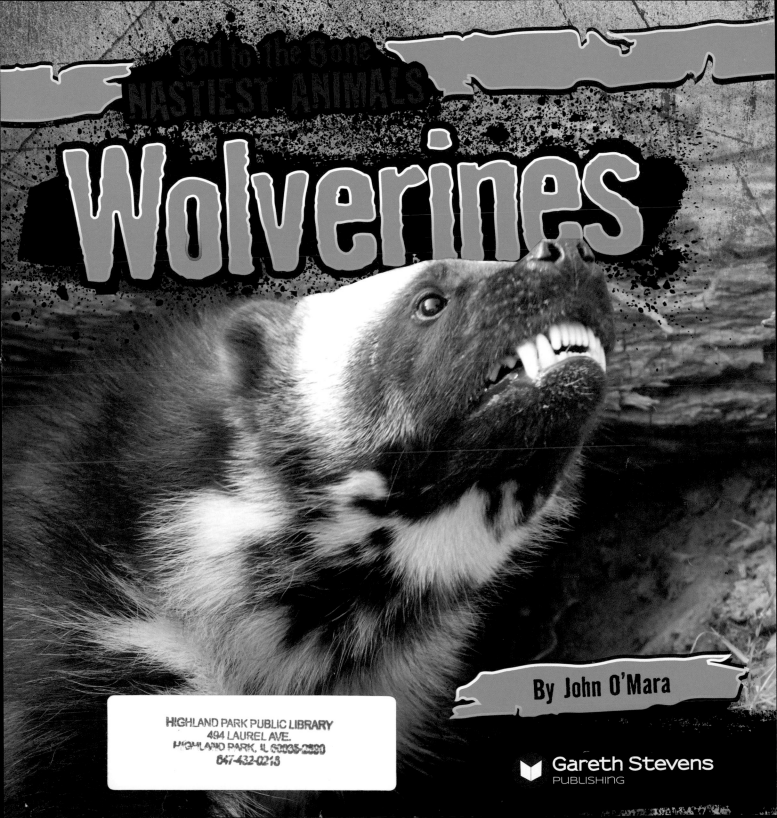

Bad to the Bone
NASTIEST ANIMALS

Wolverines

By John O'Mara

Gareth Stevens
PUBLISHING

Please visit our website, www.garethstevens.com. For a free color catalog of all our high-quality books, call toll free 1-800-542-2595 or fax 1-877-542-2596.

Library of Congress Cataloging-in-Publication Data

O'Mara, John.
 Wolverines / John O'Mara.
    pages cm. — (Bad to the bone, Nasty animals)
 Includes index.
 ISBN 978-1-4824-1970-2 (pbk.)
 ISBN 978-1-4824-1969-6 (6 pack)
 ISBN 978-1-4824-1971-9 (library binding)
 1. Wolverine—Juvenile literature. I. Title.
 QL737.C25O53 2015
 599.76'6—dc23

                                        2014032726

First Edition

Published in 2015 by
Gareth Stevens Publishing
111 East 14th Street, Suite 349
New York, NY 10003

Copyright © 2015 Gareth Stevens Publishing

Designer: Michael Flynn and Laura Bowen
Editor: Therese Shea

Photo credits: Cover, p. 1 Robert Postma/First Light/Getty Images; cover, pp. 1–24 (series art) foxie/Shutterstock.com; cover, pp. 1–24 (series art) Larysa Ray/Shutterstock.com; cover, pp. 1–24 (series art) LeksusTuss/Shutterstock.com; p. 5 Zefram/Wikipedia.com; p. 7 (world map) Nelson Marques/Shutterstock.com; p. 7 (wolverine) Nazzu/Shutterstock.com; pp. 9, 19 Daniel J. Cox/Oxford Scientific/Getty Images; p. 11 Anna Yu/E+/Getty Images; p. 13 Mark Hamblin/Oxford Scientific/Getty Images; p. 15 Juan Carlos Munoz/age fotostock/Getty Images; p. 17 Michal Ninger/Shutterstock.com; p. 21 Erik Mandre/Shutterstock.com.

Printed in the United States of America

CPSIA compliance information: Batch #CW15GS: For further information contact Gareth Stevens, New York, New York at 1-800-542-2595.

Contents

Words in the glossary appear in **bold** type the first time they are used in the text.

Hungry, Hungry Wolverine

Strong, fearless, clever—these are words used to describe the predator called the wolverine. Most of all, it's hungry. If you went to dinner with a wolverine, it would have trouble choosing from the **menu**—because it eats everything! But you wouldn't want to get that close to a wolverine. It has no problem attacking animals much larger than itself.

Wolverines may not be big, but they have some useful **weapons** for surviving in the wild. These are special **adaptations** that together make the wolverine a scary predator.

That's Nasty!

The wolverine's scientific name is *Gulo gulo*. *Gulo* is Latin for "gluttony." "Gluttony" means "eating too much"!

Other names for the wolverine are glutton, carcajou, and skunk bear.

It's a Weasel!

Wolverines aren't bears, though they look a bit like them. They're not wolves, either. They're the largest member of the weasel family! Wolverines have a long-haired coat that's usually blackish brown. They have a "mask" of lighter-colored hair on their face. A light brown stripe usually runs from each shoulder to the tail.

Wolverines are usually 26 to 36 inches (66 to 91 cm) long, with a bushy tail adding about another 10 inches (25 cm). A wolverine's shoulders are about 18 inches (46 cm) high. It may weigh more than 40 pounds (18 kg).

North
America

South
America

Europe

Asia

Africa

Australia

wolverine habitats

Wolverines like to live in cold, wooded **habitats**
that receive a lot of snow year-round.

A Killer Appetite

A wolverine has five long, sharp, curved claws on each foot. It uses these for fighting, digging, and climbing steep surfaces. A wolverine also has large, strong teeth and powerful jaws. These help it kill and eat its prey—even the prey's bones!

A wolverine mostly hunts for food at night. It may walk as many as 40 miles (64 km) a day in its search. It uses its senses of smell and hearing to find prey wandering around its habitat.

That's Nasty!

Wolverines will attack larger animals, especially if the animals are sick or hurt.

A wolverine has short ears,
but a very good sense of hearing.

Lots on the Menu

You'd never say a wolverine is a picky eater. Plants and berries are on the menu in the summer, but wolverines are always hungry for meat. They eat rabbits and **rodents**, but have no problem attacking larger animals, such as sheep, deer, **caribou**, and even small bears.

Wolverines are scavengers, too. That means they eat dead animals and other predators' leftovers. Wolverines sometimes even dig into underground dens to find something to eat.

That's Nasty!

A rotting dead animal is called carrion. Carrion is one of the wolverine's favorite treats when there's less to eat in winter.

A wolverine is an omnivore. That means it eats plants and animals.

Snowshoe Feet

Scientists think wolverines like living in snowy places because they're specially built to find things to eat in winter. In winter, wolverine feet are covered with stiff hair that helps them walk on top of deep snow! However, wolverines can use their claws to quickly dig through the snow if they smell a snack beneath it.

Rodents make tunnels under the snow. Deer and other animals sometimes can't find enough to eat and die in winter. Wolverines can find their **carcasses** in the snow, too.

That's Nasty!

A wolverine's sense of smell can find a carcass lying 20 feet (6.1 m) under the snow!

Wolverines use their sense of smell
to locate animals in deep snow.

What's That Smell?

Wolverines earned one of their other names—skunk bear. Somewhat like a skunk sprays a stinky liquid to protect itself, a wolverine can **release** a "stink bomb"! Wolverines have body parts called glands on their bottom from which the smelly liquid comes.

Wolverines release this liquid to mark their territory. They don't like other wolverines in their territory, so the smell tells them to stay away. They may also release the smelly matter on their food so other animals don't want to steal it from them!

A wolverine may wait in a tree and jump on top of its prey.

15

Anything for a Meal

Wolverines use their deadly fighting skills for many reasons. They fight to bring down their prey. They also fight to keep other animals away from their food. After it kills something large, a wolverine may drag it to a cave to guard the carcass until it can eat. A wolverine can drag something five times heavier than itself!

Sometimes, to get a really big meal, wolverines wait for a bear or other animal to kill something. Then, they try to steal it away by growling or showing their sharp teeth.

That's Nasty!

One report says that a 30-pound (14 kg) wolverine tried to steal food from a 400-pound (182 kg) black bear!

This wolverine is trying to scare off an enemy. You can tell it's a meat eater by its teeth!

Baby Beasts

Wolverines like a snowy habitat because that's where they hide their babies. Mother wolverines dig dens in the snow and have one to five babies each year between January and April. The baby wolverines drink their mother's milk at first. They grow very fast.

By the time the baby wolverines are 4 months old, they're ready to go out in the wild to find food for themselves. They're usually fully grown by the time they're 1 year old.

Wolverine babies are called kits or cubs.

Tracking Wolverines

The only animals that hunt the wolverine are people! People hunt them because wolverines grow such a thick fur coat in winter. People use wolverine fur for warm clothing.

Scientists hunt wolverines, too, but not to hurt them. Wolverines are very hard to study in the wild. Scientists have set up cameras to see them. They've also attached radios to some wolverines so they can track their movements. Hopefully, someday we'll know much more about these nasty—but important—wild animals.

sharp teeth

excellent senses of
smell and hearing

powerful jaws

Wolverines: So Nasty!

long, sharp claws

nasty smell

fight animals much
larger than they are

Wolverines usually live 7 to 12 years in the wild.

Glossary

adaptation: a change in a type of animal that makes it better able to live in its surroundings

carcass: the dead body of an animal

caribou: reindeer

habitat: the natural place where an animal or plant lives

menu: a list of foods available to eat

release: to let go

rodent: a small, furry animal with large front teeth, such as a mouse or rat

weapon: something used to cause injury or death

For More Information

Books

de la Bédoyère, Camilla. *Deadly Predators*. Mankato, MN: QEB Publishing, 2013.

Markovics, Joyce. *Wolverine: Super Strong*. New York, NY: Bearport Publishing, 2011.

Quinlan, Julia J. *Wolverines*. New York, NY: PowerKids Press, 2013.

Websites

Wolverine
kids.nationalgeographic.com/animals/wolverine.html
Find great photos of wolverines and other animals here.

The Wolverine Foundation: Kid's Page
wolverinefoundation.org/kids-page/551-2
If you have more questions about wolverines, check out this site.